THE RULING CLAWSS

SYD HOFF was born in the Bronx, New York. He sold his first cartoon to *The New Yorker* at age 18 and went on to publish more than 500 cartoons in the magazine, becoming known for his depictions of lower-middle-class life in New York City. Beginning in 1933 and ending in the 1940s, Hoff contributed cartoons to leftist magazines such as *New Masses* and the *Daily Worker* under the pen name "A. Redfield" in order to conceal his political sympathies.

PHILIP NEL is University Distinguished Professor of English at Kansas State University. He is the author or coeditor of thirteen books, including *Was the Cat in the Hat Black?: The Hidden Racism of Children's Literature, and the Need for Diverse Books* (2017).

THIS IS A NEW YORK REVIEW COMIC
PUBLISHED BY THE NEW YORK REVIEW OF BOOKS
207 East 32nd Street
New York, NY 10016
www.nyrb.com/comics

Cover design by Brian McMullen

Library of Congress Cataloging-in-Publication Data

Names: Redfield, A., 1912-2004, author.
Title: The ruling clawss / A. Redfield.
Other titles: Daily worker.
Identifiers: LCCN 2022029490 | ISBN 9781681377414 (paperback)
Subjects: LCSH: Upper class--United States--Caricatures and cartoons. |
    Working class--United States--Caricatures and cartoons.
Classification: LCC NC1429.R425 A4 2023 | DDC 741.5/6973--dc23/
eng/20220915
LC record available at https://lccn.loc.gov/2022029490

ISBN: 978-1-68137-741-4

Printed in the United States of America

10 9 8 7 6 5 4 3 2 1

THE

RULING CLAWSS

BY
REDFIELD

THE SOCIALIST CARTOONS OF
SYD HOFF

Introduction by Philip Nel

Original Introduction by
ROBERT FORSYTHE

Afterword by
REDFIELD

New York   NEW YORK REVIEW COMICS   2023

Comrade Redfield & Mr. Hoff

Syd Hoff. Undated photograph included in Melvin L. Heimer's *Famous Artists and Writers of King Features Syndicate* (King Features Syndicate, Inc., 1946).

Introduction by Philip Nel

This is Syd Hoff's first book. It may also be his least-known book. There are three reasons for its relative obscurity.

First, a collection of cartoons issued by a 1930s Communist newspaper did not enjoy the wide distribution of a book printed by a major American publisher.

Hoff's most popular book, the children's classic *Danny and the Dinosaur* (Harper, 1958), sold over ten million copies, and was translated into a dozen languages.

This edition of *The Ruling Clawss* marks its first reprinting. It was published in December 1935 by the *Daily Worker*, the official newspaper of the Communist Party USA and the place where these cartoons initially appeared. The print run was small and its audience limited to Americans who believed in international socialism.

The second reason this is a lesser-known Syd Hoff book is that it's one of only two he published under the pseudonym "A. Redfield."

Though most on the Left used the same name for all of their work, adopting a pen name for radical work was not unheard of. Robert Forsythe, the author of this book's original introduction, was actually Kyle Crichton (1896–1960)—playwright, journalist, and editor at *Collier's Weekly*.

According to Hoff, Clarence Hathaway was the source of both the "Redfield" pseudonym and the cartoon's name. Having risen through the ranks of the Communist Party alongside its leader Earl Browder, Hathaway had just become editor of the *Daily Worker*. Understanding that cartoons distill ideas into a visual language that can reach and persuade more readers, he brought Hoff on as a contributing cartoonist. "The Ruling Clawss" ran from 1933 to 1935.[1]

The third reason you may not know about the A. Redfield work is that Hoff didn't want you to. After telling me some of the above information in an August 2000 letter, Hoff drew an arrow to it, and added: "These remarks should not be printed because they'd destroy me as a 'children's author!' Please refrain!"[2]

I had written him for memories of Crockett Johnson—creator of the comic strip *Barnaby* (1942–1952) and the children's book *Harold and the Purple Crayon* (1955)—whose biography I had just begun writing. Syd's first letter to me began, "Old age is memories, of course, and I remember so much, not only Crockett J., my old editor at the *New Masses*, but Butch Limbach who inherited the job." Mistaking me for someone of his generation, he concluded that first letter with an invitation to visit him in Florida: "We'll have a great time remembering."[3]

Though he remembered these formative years well, biographical sketches published during Hoff's life omit his A. Redfield work, alleging that Hoff's first collection of cartoons is *Feeling No Pain* (Dial, 1944) and not *Ruling Clawss*, published nine years earlier. They claim *Muscles and Brains* (Dial, 1940) as his first children's book, rather than Redfield's *Mr. His*, published in 1939 by the weekly communist magazine *New Masses*.

In a statement he made to the FBI in 1952, Hoff downplayed his A. Redfield cartoons, joining the staff of the *Daily Worker*, and any other work he did for CPUSA-affiliated or -adjacent groups. "My association with the 'Daily Worker' and 'New Masses', the Young Communist League and the American League against War and Fascism was all based . . . on a lack of knowledge or experience as to what they actually stood for," he wrote. "I do not now or did not in the past at any time espouse the doctrine of Communism as I now know it," Hoff assured the FBI.[4]

The truth is a bit more complicated.

It begins in a three-room apartment in the Bronx, where, in September 1912, Sydney Hoffberg was born to Mary, a homemaker, and Ben Hoffberg, a dry goods salesman. There, he joined brother Danny, two years his senior. Eight years later, younger sister Dorothy would complete the family. Danny became Hoff's "great protector from bullies" and is the reason that, decades later, Hoff named the dinosaur's friend "Danny" in his children's book. Fascinated by pictures, Hoff began making his own at the age of four: "I began drawing with coal on the back of a shovel, just like Abe Lincoln. There, the resemblance to Lincoln ends."[5]

Though there were no artists in the family, his mother encouraged his interest. Returning home after a trolley-car ride, Hoff "drew a picture of the conductor, resplendent in his uniform with brass buttons." As he recalled to me years later, his mother then "proclaimed" that "Sydney is the artist of the family," and began "immediately hammering the picture into the wall with a three-inch nail."[6]

At about the same age, Hoff drew his first political cartoon. "In 1917, during World War One, I remember drawing Kaiser Wilhelm's likeness in the gutter with chalk. When I finished, all the boys would pee Germany's leader off the face of the earth, while the whole street cheered."[7]

His other early subjects—all drawn on paper—included his extended Russian-Polish Jewish family, the working-class neighborhood where they lived, movies he and his brother saw, and newspaper comics. He copied his favorites: Winsor McCay's Little Nemo, Bud Fisher's Mutt and Jeff, Frederick Opper's Happy Hooligan, Rube Goldberg's Boob McNutt, and his favorite, Harry Hershfield's Abie the Agent.[8]

He got good at drawing. When cartoonist Milt Gross was announced as a guest at an upcoming high school assembly, Hoff's art teacher enlisted Hoff to draw as part of the entertainment. After Gross had given his talk and drawn a few of his famous characters, a member of the drama club gave a speech on "The History of Locomotion," while Hoff illustrated it in real time. As he recalled, "The moment I finished, Milt Gross leaped to my side and embraced me. 'Kid, someday you'll be a great cartoonist!' he proclaimed, loud enough for the whole school to hear. Later, he made a sketch in my notebook, while everyone was begging him for autographs. It was all like a dream."[9]

A talented artist but an indifferent student, Hoff dropped out of high school at the age of fifteen. He had already worked part-time as a soda-jerk, a bus boy, and a copy boy at the New York Daily News. Thinking that painting billboards might be his full-time job, he enrolled in a course on sign-painting. When he finished the course, he got a job not painting signs, but instead making wood-and-sheet-metal sign frames. Hoff had "never been handy," and "it didn't take the boss very long to notice that most of my hammering was on my fingernails. He delayed firing me long enough to have me decorate a friend's nightclub with pictures of dancing girls."[10]

After Hoff failed as a sign painter, his father suggested he try bricklaying. His mother advised him to become a plumber. His brother, Danny, who was by then a cab driver, thought Hoff should develop his artistic talent. He drove him to the National Academy of Design, and told him: "You're always drawing, now learn how." Claiming that he was 16 years old (he was still 15), Hoff filled out an application, and started class the next day. Though his father was not enthusiastic about his son's career choice, he gave Hoff a small allowance, Danny contributed tips from his cab-driving, and Hoff got a job as an usher at a movie theater.[11]

At the Academy, Boris Gorelick—a former high school classmate—introduced Hoff to the

Syd Hoff

THEY HATE TO SEE A WORKING MAN DONATE A DOLLAR

But a strike is news, and generally appears in shrieking headlines—and, of course, they say labor is always to blame.

The fact is that, since Pearl Harbor, only one-tenth of one per cent of man-hours have been lost by strikes. Can you beat that! But you know even those candidates who burst out in election-year, election-year affection for social legislation and for labor in general, still think that you ought to be good boys and stay out of politics. And above all, they hate to see any working man or woman contribute a dollar bill to any wicked political party.

Of course, it's all right for the large financiers and industrialists and monopolists to contribute tens of thousands of dollars—but their solicitude for that dollar which the men and women in the ranks of labor contribute is always very touching.

Hoff's contribution to "The President's Speech Illustrated by Nineteen Artists." FDR's speech to the Teamsters Union on Sept. 23rd 1944, issued by the Independent Voters Committee of the Arts and Sciences for Roosevelt, and featuring artwork by William Gropper, Crockett Johnson, Lynd Ward, Hoff and others.

A Day in the Life of der Führer

A. Redfield, "A Day in the Life of der Führer," New Masses, 29 Nov. 1938. Image from Marxist Internet Archive.

Communist movement. As Hoff recalled, Gorelick

was hurrying out of the Academy one day, just when the New York *Daily News* was having...front page words and photos of "Red" meetings in Union Square, NYC, with mounted police attacking protesters, etc. "Where ya going, Boris?" I asked innocently, "to one of them Red meetings?" He gave me an answer I never forgot: "Don't you know, a Russian tree is just like an American tree?" Sounds funny, but in one second, I had a universal feeling.

When the Depression hit, Hoff's father lost 40 percent of his savings. At the same time, Hoff himself was beginning to find success as a professional cartoonist. In 1930, *The New Yorker* bought a small cartoon of his—the first of 571 he would publish there. Within a few years, his cartoons were also appearing in other magazines.[12]

As the Depression continued, Hoff grew politically active. When the Cartoonists Guild (of which Hoff was a member) realized that the magazine *College Humor* was paying below scale, he and other guild members picketed their offices. "An officer materialized out of thin air and we found ourselves being hauled off to the Forty-seventh Street police station on a charge of 'obstructing pedestrian traffic.' In our cells we sang 'Solidarity Forever.'" They were released that evening, but the arrests made the news.[13]

He joined the John Reed Club, a group of leftist artists, writers, and intellectuals—many of whom were Communists. He went to Camp Unity, a CPUSA-affiliated, racially integrated summer resort. There, he met Abel Meeropol, who would go on to write the 1937 anti-lynching anthem "Strange Fruit." Hoff recalled: "Meeropol once begged me to advise him how to get into the movement...[but he] didn't need any advice." A natural activist, Meeropol in the 1950s adopted the orphaned sons of Julius and Ethel Rosenberg. Hoff and fellow New Yorker illustrator Abe Birnbaum painted a mural at Cafe Society, the integrated Greenwich Village nightclub where Billie Holiday first sang "Strange Fruit."[14]

When Hathaway brought him on the staff of the Daily Worker in 1933, Hoff—as Redfield—published cartoons there, and in New Masses, Young Communist Review, Champion of Youth, and March of Labor. He served as art director for New Pioneer, the magazine of the Young Pioneers—the Communist version of the Boy Scouts and Girl Scouts.[15]

In a July 2000 letter to me, he wrote with great feeling about "marching in a May Day Parade with beloved comrades":

> [Alfred] Hayes, author of The Girl on the Via Flaminia, ... was right in step with me, as well as Greg Duncan, an artist who lived long enough to become an Ernest Hemingway illustrator, then died in [the Battle of] Anzio, WWII.... Lewis Merrill, founder of the Union for Office Workers, was in the ranks, as well as Joe Curran of the Stevedores Union made famous by [Budd] Schulberg and Elia Kazan [in On the Waterfront].

He concluded, "I recall sadly many old friends taking off at the Hudson River, with the Lincoln Brigade"—the American leftists who in 1937 fought against Franco in the Spanish Civil War.

Hoff added, "I was dying to go myself, but my mother probably saved my life with her high blood pressure."[16]

Since Hoff remembered these names when he wrote to me in 2000, he certainly knew them a half-century earlier. But, in his statement to the FBI in 1952, he was wisely forgetful. Noting that he had "been asked for the names and identities" of people he knew via the Daily Worker and other leftist groups, Hoff claimed, "I do not recall the names of any of the people for the reason that this period of my life goes back ten to twelve years and, further, even at that time my connection with them was so casual that I made no friends or close acquaintances."[17]

He named two people—Clarence Hathaway and Russell "Butch" Limbach—whose names were easily found on the masthead of Communist-aligned publications and thus were already known to the FBI. Indeed, Hathaway's public expulsion from the CPUSA made headlines in 1941. As if to emphasize a poor memory, Hoff spelled Limbach as "Limback," misidentifying him as the art editor of New Masses and "the man with whom I dealt and sent material to." When Hoff contributed, the art editor was Crockett Johnson.[18]

Hoff need not have dissembled. The FBI, the House Committee on Un-American Activities, and Senator Joseph McCarthy mostly did not bother writers for young people. As Julia Mickenberg's Learning from the Left (2006) documents, many blacklisted writers found work writing for children because, during the Cold War, "there was no blacklist per se in children's publishing." Seeing children's books as a field dominated by women, anti-Communist zealots deemed it less important and largely ignored it.[19]

But Hoff could not have known that his profession would be spared this scrutiny. As he saw people he knew called to testify or get blacklisted, he doubtless wondered whether he would be next. The method of blacklisting encouraged anxiety. There was no official list. Instead, you suddenly found your book contracts cancelled, your invitation to speak rescinded, people no longer returning your calls, and with no way to defend your reputation.

Hoff began his letter to the FBI noting that he was writing "of my own free will" and that "no threats or promises of any kind have been made to me in order to make this statement." However, an implicit threat hung over the heads of anyone associated with the Communist movement. As Hoff explained, "My purpose in making this statement to the FBI is to clarify the record, . . . since it has come to my attention recently that I am being accused of publishing certain cartoons and drawings of a subversive nature." To clear his name, Hoff strove to assert the maximum amount of distance between the loyal citizen he had become and the radical Redfield he had been.[20]

In the early 1940s, Hoff retired the A. Redfield pseudonym. Perhaps there's some truth to the explanation he gave the FBI: "Not long after the summer of 1935, the girl with whom I was keeping company and whom I later married influenced me against my running around and being associated with Communists and Communist organizations." The timing suggests that this was not the sole reason: He married Dora ("Dutch") Berman in 1937 and kept publishing as Redfield until at least 1940. Perhaps he had grown weary of party politics. Perhaps his busy (and better-paying) career as a professional cartoonist left him little time for other pursuits. Quite likely, all of the above.[21]

He created the syndicated comic Tuffy (1939– 1949), which would appear in over 800 newspapers—distributed by Hearst, whose conservative politics and sensationalist newspapers Hoff deplored. Declared "essential for the national morale," Tuffy kept Hoff out of active military duty. He drew cartoons for the Office of War Information that were dropped behind enemy lines. Hoff also contributed cartoons to Artists

Against the Axis, a touring exhibit that raised money for war bonds and featured some of the best cartoonists in the US: Charles Addams, Peter Arno, William Gropper, Crockett Johnson, Ad Reinhardt, Carl Rose, and Saul Steinberg.[22]

Across his long career, Hoff drew countless cartoons for magazines, created the long-running Laugh It Off cartoon (1958– 1977), and wrote books for both adults and children. Danny and the Dinosaur, his first book written for legendary Harper editor Ursula Nordstrom's "I Can Read!" series, launched his most prolific period in the field of children's literature. He would write over 100 books for young readers, including Sammy the Seal (1959), Julius (1959), Chester (1961), Stanley (1962), and The Horse in Harry's Room (1970).

Though most of his later works do not hint at his earlier radicalism, a few remind us that Hoff was once Redfield. His children's book Boss Tweed and the Man Who Drew Him (1978) tells how Thomas Nast's cartoons helped end the reign of the corrupt politician William Marcy Tweed in nineteenth-century New York. Echoing A. Redfield's more sharply worded cartooning manifesto (in his afterword to The Ruling Clawss), Hoff in his Editorial Cartooning: From Earliest Times to the Present (1976) contends that an effective political cartoonist "can play on readers' emotions, causing them to feel shock, fear, anger, amusement, despair and moral indignation, so that they might want to take to the streets, brandish placards, and maybe march on Washington."[23]

While I don't know whether the cartoons of The Ruling Clawss had or will have such an effect, they remain surprisingly current. Update the visual iconography, and many of these could run today. Just change those fat capitalists in formal wear into tech bros in jeans and a t-shirt. We'd also draw a more diverse world. In present-day political cartoons, workers and executives would not solely be men, couples not exclusively heterosexual, and Russia not idealized as a socialist workers' utopia (see especially the cartoon on page 61, in which Hoff has incorporated Russian signage that translates to "Workers' Café" and "Factory-Kitchen No. 1"). To his credit, Hoff does avoid caricature in his drawing of the Pullman porter (page 124)—the sole Black character in this collection. And two of the cartoons (38, 44) call attention to racism.

Since the concerns of the 1930s have returned in the 2020s, it's fortunate that Hoff's take on them speaks as much to his time as to ours. The repetition, in the 2020s, that we're living through "unprecedented" times turns us away from the histories and knowledge that would help us face our present crises. Hoff's cartoons not only show us precedents, but invite us to join the struggle.

When a jailor, keys in hand, says through the bars to the unseen prisoner, "So, ya believe in the Constitution, eh?" (page 74), Hoff reminds us of our Constitutional rights to freedom of speech, of the press, and of assembly—rights too often ignored by a police and military that serve the powerful, another theme of Hoff's Redfield work. In what may be the most acid cartoon in this entire collection, a rich couple pause before a legless veteran while the wife says, "Give him a nickel, sweetheart. After all, you made a couple of million on the war" (109). Here and in other cartoons, Hoff challenges those "patriots" who profit from war while remaining indifferent to its human costs.

When a well-fed diner at a lush banquet insists that "anybody who says there's starvation in America ought to have his head examined" (page 60) or a plump matron instructs her thin maid to feed the goldfish "every day while I'm away—we don't want any cases of malnutrition in THIS family" (92), Hoff highlights the persistence of a food insecurity that could be addressed if the wealthy paid their fair share of taxes. When he shows elite pets being treated like royalty (pages 23, 42, 141, 150), Hoff prompts us to ask why such excessive wealth is not shared with the millions of humans unable to meet even their most basic needs.

When a tuxedoed gent tells the elegant woman next to him, "Papa says if I'm expelled from one more college I'll have to take charge of one of his factories" (page 56), Hoff calls attention to children of the rich being allowed to fail upwards—a still contemporary phenomenon embodied in the 45th president of the US, who promoted the myth that he was a self-made billionaire. Another Hoff cartoon speaks directly to Trump's lie that his father's "small loan of a million dollars" helped him start his business (it was actually at least $413 million). In Hoff's cartoon, a wealthy man tells his son, "It was the usual story of from rags to riches with me, Junior—your grandfather died, leaving me only a half-million" (page 165).[24]

Laughter lets us know we are not alone: someone else understands our predicament. And, in that understanding, Hoff's cartoons suggest, we can build solidarity, organize, and fight for a better future.

The characters in these cartoons take to the streets, marching "AGAINST IMPERIALIST WAR" (page 24), striking for better working conditions (54), and demanding "UNEMPLOYMENT INSURANCE" (72). They are an invitation to look up from our doomscrolling, wrest ourselves away from the addictive anesthetic of social media, and take action.

The oligarchs of today's "Ruling Clawss" are just as dangerous, and I understand why our many and proliferating challenges may beget gloom. But, as the activists in these cartoons (and the activist who drew them) might point out, despair only aids the oppressor. If we assume defeat, we consent to our ongoing diminishment. If we fight back, we have a chance of creating a society in which the many can flourish. Here's hoping that contemporary readers of these cartoons take that chance, link arms with Hoff's marchers, and accept their invitation to build a better world.

1. Syd Hoff, letter to author, 1 Aug. 2000; Sydney Hoff, statement to FBI, 22 Dec. 1952, Hoff's FBI file; Paul Buhle, "Daily Worker," *Encyclopedia of the American Left*, p. 175.

3. Hoff, letter to author, 1 Aug. 2022.

4. Hoff, letter to author, 8 July 2000.

5. Hoff, statement to FBI, 22 Dec. 1952.

6. Carol Edmonton, "Home Is Where the Gefilte Fish Is," *Syd Hoff: Cartoonist & Author* <http://www.sydhoff.org/pages/exhibit.html>; Syd Hoff, "Autobiography," *Something About the Author: Autobiography Series*, ed. Joyce Nakamura, (Gale, 1987), repr. on *Syd Hoff: Cartoonist & Author* <http://www.sydhoff.org/pages/about.html>; Mel Heimer, "Syd Hoff," *Famous Artists and Writers of King Features Syndicate* (King Features, 1946), n.p.

7. Hoff, "Autobiography."

8. Hoff, "Autobiography."

9. Edmonton, "Home Is Where the Gefilte Fish Is"; Hoff, "Autobiography."

10. Hoff, "Autobiography."

11. Hoff, "Autobiography."

12. Hoff, "Autobiography."

13. Edmonton, "Home Is Where the Gefilte Fish Is"; Hoff, "Autobiography."

14. Hoff, "Autobiography."

15. Hoff, letter to author, 15 July 2000.

16. Carol Edmonton, "Syd Hoff – TIME LINE"; Paul Mishler, *Raising Reds: The Young Pioneers, Radical Summer Camps, and Communist Political Culture in the United States* (Columbia UP), pp. 41-42.

17. Hoff, letter to author, 15 July 2000.

18. Hoff, statement to FBI, 22 Dec. 1952.

19. Hoff, letter to author, 8 July 2000.

20. Julia Mickenberg, *Learning from the Left: Children's Literature, the Cold War, and Radical Politics in the United States* (Oxford UP, 2006), pp. 15, 142.

21. Hoff, statement to FBI, 22 Dec. 1952.

22. Hoff, statement to FBI, 22 Dec. 1952.

23. Hoff, "Autobiography"; Nel, *Crockett Johnson and Ruth Krauss: How an Unlikely Couple Found Love, Dodged the FBI, and Transformed Children's Literature* (UP Mississippi, 2012), p. 58.

24. Hoff, *Editorial and Political Cartooning: From Earliest Times to the Present* (Stravon, 1976), p. 13.

25. David Barstow, Susanne Craig and Russ Buettner, "Trump Engaged in Suspect Tax Schemes as He Reaped Riches From His Father," *New York Times*, 2 Oct. 2018.

AMERICA

A. Redfield, "Hearst / New Declaration of Independence." 16 July 1935. Image from Marxist Internet Archive.

Introduction
Robert Forsythe (1935)

With the desire we all have to act as God, I have tried to convince myself that I invented Redfield, but since I have only seen the man once and had nothing whatever to do with his start on the *Daily Worker*, I can comfort myself only with the fact that we are spiritual blood-brothers.

For me to say that he is a fine satiric artist is to repeat only what the pictures themselves tell you. Of his background I know nothing. He may draw his ponderous-paunched females out of a sense of hatred accumulated through years as an elevator man in a Park Avenue apartment house, but this hardly seems likely. To a man of Redfield's apparent good sense, it would be extremely foolish to waste good rage over people as fundamentally ass-like as these. What actuates him, obviously, is a feeling of relief and gratitude and superiority. In great part, superiority.

The arrogance of the proletariat is always a source of concern to the upper classes. Acting upon the assumption that their eminence in life constitutes a condition about which the rest of the world should be envious, they are perpetually nonplussed at discovering that the workers, and particularly the revolutionary artists, consider them not objects of envy but subjects of great comic importance. The most casual examination of the Redfield drawings will convince one that far from being awed by the horrendous ladies and gentlemen, he is in a constant state of hilarity over them.

What the workers resent about the rich is not their wealth but the fact that they constitute a severe reflection upon the human race. I am constantly coming upon individuals so profoundly and elaborately grotesque as to drive the most radical cartoonist out of his head. Because Charles Dana Gibson and John Held, Jr., created whole generations of fantastic human beings, we are prone to believe that such men as Daumier and Robert Minor and Art Young and Redfield have done as much for the fabulous creatures we may see any evening of the week dining at such a place as the Hotel Plaza in New York City. There they sit–the women bejeweled, the men bejowled. You could no more be envious of such a horrible spectacle than you could be envious of Hauptmann because his exploits have been chronicled upon the front pages of the newspapers. The idea that you could invent these people is ridiculous; no human mind is capable of such transcendental imagination.

The appearance of Redfield's drawings in the *Daily Worker* is peculiarly fortunate for both. If upon occasion I speak harshly of such periodicals as *The New Yorker* and *Life*, it is with more sorrow than anger. At bottom, as must be clear, I have high regard for the capabilities of the ladies and gentlemen who conduct those magazines. What saddens me is the shocking disregard they have for their own talents and reputations. Redfield is a superior satirist; what makes him an outstanding figure is the material with which he deals. Approaching the problem of public conduct from exactly the same level at which it is attacked by most of the present-day artists, he brings to his work an incisiveness which is not possible in even the more sophisticated general magazines and newspapers. The fact of a social point of view makes not only a more satisfied creator but obviously a more capable artist. Because I am a writer and have the usual guilty feeling that we are all rather bad characters, I may give too much credit to the good intentions and warm hearts of the artists, but the recent satiric issue of the *New Masses* (made possible by the brilliant labors of Gardner Rea) with contributions by the best of the cartoonists who regularly appear in more lofty publications seems an indication of the realization of the point I have been making. At the very least, it shows they are not afraid.

I suppose it is true that Redfield is a revolutionary rather than a proletariat artist. Whether the distinction means anything, I don't know. What I am trying to say is that there are artists and writers who are good on attack–Jacob Burck, Phil Bard, Michael Gold, Joseph Freedman, Granville Hicks–and others, like Redfield and myself, who are strictly counter-fighters. Although my own back-

16

ground is proletarian—coal mines and steel work—I have lived so long in another way of life that it would be nonsensical of me to attempt a proletarian novel, for example. What I can do, and what Redfield is doing so superbly, is hack away at the vicious old existence with such weapons as we have at our command. In short, every man to his last. There are those who can build a new world and those who can help tear down the old. What makes Vincent Sheehan's *PERSONAL HISTORY* one of the most important books of our time is his realization of this truth. We may be so constructed that we are incapable of certain things which must be done in making a revolution but we can do what we CAN do. It may be a great deal, it may be very little, but we can do it. If nothing more, we can think straight.

Redfield has found his way and the *Daily Worker* has the good sense to help him pursue it. The fact that he uses a bourgeois technique for revolutionary ends has been criticized. I can think of nothing of less importance. If he preferred standing on his head and doing his work in the Rube Goldberg manner, it would be entirely all right with me. What he is doing is reflecting the honest disdain of the workers for the pathetic upper classes. This attitude is not forced in the slightest. Historically regarded, there is no more doubt of the triumph of the proletariat than of the sun-rise. It has been established practically in the Soviet Union; philosophically and culturally, it has gained ascendancy everywhere. No artist in his straight mind would think of linking his fortunes with the specimens which now pass as our aristocracy.

But this is too ponderous for a discussion of drawings which are so biting and cauterizing and delightful as these. The delight, I am afraid, is all on our side, but even the gorgeous half-wits who cut the wages and prepare themselves fatuously for fascism get some pleasure out of realizing they can be so awesomely ridiculous. In a sense, they are a triumph. A triumph of matter over mind, of course; but a triumph.

—Robert Forsythe

Dec. 2, 1935

"Fellow workers..."

"How the hell many times must I ring for you?"

"Please, Vivian...show a little discretion..."

"I ain't afraid of nothing!"

"We are here, Madame."

"Good morning, sir."
"What the hell's good about it?"

"Can you imagine? I dreamt I was a working girl..."

"Ah, Berlin! So quiet—so calm—so serene."

"Well! Well! Well! And how's
the Giant of Wall Street today?"

"Poor fellow... I'd like to see you go straight—
how'd you like a job as a strike-breaker?"

"And gweat big, thugar daddy'll give itty
bitsy snookums a check account all of her own."

"A raise? Who the hell are you supporting?"

"With feeling, Mrs. Gould—
you're expressing the Spirit of
Charity casting crumbs to the poor."

"This is a hot one on mother—
ME taking HER gigolo away!"

"The Generalissimo just got a splinter in
his finger.... How's things at the front?"

"So you're showing off your college
education again, eh, Hooligan?
I hear you say 'excuse me' whenever
you bang a picket!"

"I can hardly wait for the new war—
it was such fun last time knitting socks
and wrapping bandages."

"I'm so glad that you're a family man—I hate to pay thirteen dollars a week to just ANYONE."

"Some of my best friends are scabs."

"I can't forget the last lynching—I still
have a hoarse throat from cheering."

"Another one of our regiments'll be wiped
out here, Major, but it's all for the best."

"The cook says we haven't done a day's
work for so long, we're beginning to stink!"

"I wish mother would let me live like that
for six months so I could write a novel."

"Well, it looks like Palm Beach again this winter."

"I suppose you find the salt air
remuneration enough for your labor."

"I'm VERY sympathetic towards Negroes—
I always give one my laundry."

"Oh, judgy-wudgy! The Vice Squad had me so worried!"

"Now practice! I'll make you a genius
if I have to knock your teeth out!"

"Look, papa—everybody's crazy about my new gigolo."

"Why wouldn't he sing? His munitions
are going like hot cakes."

"Well, darling—I believe Fascism is coming."
"Oh, my!—and this is the maid's night out."

"I simply love milk, Vivian—pour in another gallon."

"Excuse me, sir—I've been working in the
shipping department thirty-one years—"
"By God! I KNEW you looked familiar!"

"...we who turn the wheels of industry..."

"You old smarty—putting
private dicks in the plant!"

"You're the only one who understands
me, Miss Scairb."

"That was delicious—I think
I'll have dinner in bed, too."

"Papa says if I'm expelled from
one more college I'll have to take
charge of one of his factories."

"I'm tired of living in a stable."

"God! What a nightmare last night! I dreamed I gave everybody a raise!"

"For the last time—KISS MAMA!"

"Anybody who says there's starvation in
America ought to have his head examined."

"I STILL don't believe it!"

"I'm against unemployment insurance—
it'd make people lazy."

"Thirty days for picketing! I'll teach
you to appreciate a free country!"

"Don't be ridiculous! Everyone
knows the depression is over!"

"Major got this one for bravery
in the Argonne—unfortunately his
regiment was wiped out."

"Heads we lay off fifty—tails we lay off a hundred."

"God, what a day! I've been clubbing
strikers for eight hours!"

"Get the hell outa here. D'ya want
people to get the impression there's
child labor in America?"

"I'm going to lunch, Miss Farber—I'm starving."

"–and ask God to make a blizzard for May Day!"

"I say the best thing is to put 'em
all on a raft and set them adrift."

"Let's hiss."

"Thank God we're both getting pensioned this month—I've just read an article on how fast a bombing plane could sink us."

"So, ya believe in the Constitution, eh?"

"Your grandfather was a victim of the
World War—he died on Wall Street."

"Yesterday was Harold's birthday—my husband
gave him a textile factory."

"Personally, I'm opposed to child labor,
but Theodore says they're less expensive."

"We must go over and feel sorry for Mrs. Syderham. Her husband just lost a strike."

"Gerald is getting promoted again—he just broke
the record for giving summonses to peddlers."

"Head up, chest out, Reggy—
we're showing the world!"

First Worker: "Intelligent looking, isn't he?"
Second Worker: "Who?"
First Worker: "The horse."

"War is not as bad as people paint it,
Mrs. Puyster—at least I haven't found it so
from my own personal experience."

"Little Phyllis worked in a department store
two days last week—isn't she heroic?"

Men working!

"By the way, honey, you'll have to resign from that pacifist organization—I bought a munition factory today."

"It says 'Unite Against Imperialist War and Fascism', Sarge—should I run him in or do we agree with him?"

THE PEEPUL'S FRIENDS
The United States Supreme Court exhibits a feat
of judicial balance and shows that our legal
system is still as solid as a pyramid (of a sort).

"Poor Rodney's vacation is ruined—his 25,000 coal miners want living conditions."

"Here's a brother in distress, Mr. Quammley—
his men are also going out on strike."

"Of course, we're all really vegetarians,
but we heard that there is a meat strike."

"Make sure they're fed every day
while I'm away—we don't want any
cases of malnutrition in THIS family."

"...and I own twenty steel mills, several railroads and steamship lines—I THINK I can support her in the manner to which she is accustomed."

"Don't forget—if Peanuts or Lefty hands
you a leaflet, call a policeman."

"Irma, you simply must be the heroine of
my new novel about the coal mines."

"I believe in free speech—WITH exceptions."

"—and in times like these we must all make sacrifices, gentlemen—let's lay off 1,200 more."

"Sister Mathilda will now reveal how Jesus
rescued her from the class struggle."

"Thanks for the injunction, Your Honor—
the strike had us worried for a little while."

"Tell everyone there'll be no vacations this year—I need a rest myself."

"The psychoanalyst suggested Europe for rest and quiet, but all I found there was picket lines, demonstrations and barricades."

"Let's fire a butler—I'm bored to death."

"Oh, boy, a demonstration today. I'm just itchin'—"

"H'y'a, Toots!"

"Get ready to clap, honey—here
comes Hitler."

"They say he owns twenty-five sweatshops
but he never perspires."

"Give him a nickel, sweetheart. After all, you
made a couple of million on the war."

"Take a peek at the factory on your way to the golf
course, Elmer—maybe some of the men are loafing."

"Nix, Casey...we can't offend the Alderman!"

"All I ask is that you do a little wage cutting
and YOU tell me they have a union!"

"Of course, the woman's problem is very simple—all she has to do is sell herself."

"Who's that?"
"Oh, his job is to see that we don't loaf."

"I've thought the whole thing over, darling,
and I'm leaving the entire estate to you."

"That reminds me—I'll be needing a new
wardrobe of minks and ermines this winter."

"I suppose those boys feel wonderful
whenever they remember they made the
world safe for democracy."

"I used to adore Mendelssohn, but I just found out he was Jewish."

"Ah, darling, without your inspiration, I could
never have developed my poison gases!"

"Oh, cookie! It's so wonderful of you to speed
up production just so I can have all this!"

"A war would be a god-send in wiping out
our over-production problem and giving us
some breathing space."

"One sees evidence of the Good
Provider everywhere."

"Should I give him a dime tip or do you think it will spoil him?"

"Opposites attract. Ambrose's company dumps thousands of gallons of milk into the river, and I dabble in milk funds."

"Lucky for him I believe in mass action."

"He was always the perfect Democrat—he
grafted equally from everybody."

"Gifford is very sentimental—he always gets a
lump in his throat whenever he fires anybody."

"Look, Humphries—the ideal type for
the union organizer."

" . . . and this is the den."

"Regular Jew hater...just like his father!"

"The day's work is done, sir."

"This meeting of the Bing Crosby Fan Club has been called to counteract the Seventh World Congress of the Communist International."

"Good morning, sir."

"Mussolini is SUCH a man—he sees something
he wants and he just takes it."

"This gives me a sense of security."

"It's all like a dream—last month I was just another college graduate and now Dad's making me vice-president of a railroad."

"Six thousand cars a day! By God, Elmer,
where do you get all your energy?"

White Guard General: "—and this is all I got left."

"Aw, baby—don't YOU start striking on me, too."

"George says the Russian Experiment will
be a failure—people have no ambition unless
they have wage cuts."

"This isn't Army Day, you dope—these people
want to take everything away from us!"

"Junior here wants to work himself up from the bottom of the ladder—he's starting as vice-president."

"Poor Grover—he's cockeyed from seeing picket lines around his factories."

"Your move, sir!"

"Run up and read the Bible to the Hogans on the third floor, Father—I'm having them dispossessed tomorrow."

"Look glum, Everett—we're supposed
to be losing money!"

"Who's winning, Hotchkiss?"
"I am, sir!"
"You're fired!"

"Hello, Magistrate Coldheart—I just
salted away another striker! That makes
us tie score!"

"Thank God he doesn't have to swim
with the dirty masses in Coney Island."

"Well, we got thirty-five guys booked for criminal syndicalism, but I still don't know what the hell it means."

"The requirements for this job are very
simple—you will be a private secretary
and—er—sort of—er—a companion."

"Representative, can we have a statement about the million families who are being taken off relief?"
"Yes—my poor heart bleeds for them."

"Poor Horace—this round the world cruise
has shown him that his coal miners function
perfectly without him."

"The Commission says it's a fire-trap, but I got pull."

"I guess the depression means nothing to you—you meet such interesting people."

"Believe me, I know what it is to go hungry—
once I didn't eat for an hour."

"I don't know what's wrong with the men, Generalissimo—they don't have the stamina for this desert sun."

"If this new cut goes through you
can have two chauffeurs."

"Aren't I lucky? Daddy says the minute the army crushes the rebellions I can go to his sugar plantations in Cuba and write poetry."

"I tell you, it's a gold mine!"

"My great-grandfather was one of the early
American settlers but I prefer gin-rickeys."

"Isn't the machine age marvelous, Honey?
All papa does is talk into the dictaphone
and presto—a hundred men are laid off!"

"To the slums, James. Edgar wants to see
the poor bathing under fire hydrants."

"It was the usual story of from rags to riches with me, Junior—your grandfather died, leaving me only a half-million."

"My God! Nothing to wear!"

"Make sure ya spell all them there letters correct."

"No doubt, if these 15,000,000 unemployed weren't so lazy they could find jobs."

"—and the first thing little Roscoe must learn
is that a worker is an inferior animal."

"On company time, huh!"

"After all, one can get along on so little."

"Aren't you exaggerating just a little
bit, Mr. Redfield?"

"Your mother must be proud..."

The Artist Says a Word About . . .

Social Satire

Some time ago I had an argument with a friend who, though he is quite reactionary, considers himself a sympathizer. That is, he feels sorry for us. He picked up a copy of *The New Yorker* and said, "Show me a single drawing in here that is not funny." I pointed out that in about twelve drawings six struck me as being quite humorous. He said, "That proves that there is such a thing as bourgeois humor." I told him I hadn't tried, and wouldn't try, to deny that there was such a thing as bourgeois humor. But I assured him that bourgeois humor had its limitations and that it was solely used by the bourgeoisie to whitewash itself. My friend leaped into the air. "What the hell do you mean?" he said. I then calmly proceeded to explain to him that society was mainly divided into two classes, an oppressed class and a class of oppressors. In general, I described the bourgeoisie as being the class in society which consciously prepares new onslaughts on the oppressed.

"But," my friend interjected, "when I want humor, I want to forget all about that. I want to forget that my position in society is insecure, and war and fascism are just around the corner. When I want to laugh I want to forget about everything." I asked him then whether he was a dope addict. He heatedly replied that he was not. I then assured him that if bourgeois humor made him "forget," dope would also, and therefore bourgeois humor is, as Marx said of religion, the opium of the masses. Picking up copies of *The New Yorker*, *Esquire*, *Judge*, *Life*, etc., I went on to show him how these publications were making a general pancake of society. That is, taking the banker boys and politicians, who are the rapers of liberty and democracy, and presenting them between perfume ads in whimsical situations. And how does the bourgeoisie make itself look human? By exposing itself in the boudoir, or the night club, doing foolish things for saying something "funny." In other words, the fascists and warmongers are little lambs who do their parts in contributing to the merriment of a nation.

My friend now "tore" into the Soviet Union. "Suppose," he demanded, "an incident happened in Russia, where a worker is the scapegoat of a joke – would Stalin print it?" I assured him that Joseph is the kind of fellow who has, at all times, the interests of the masses at heart, and that if the joke were against the working class, he would probably reject it. In fact, in the Soviet Union humor is an instrument in the hands of the working class. There, satire is used, not as a medium of escape, but as an amusing and educational means of improving the cultural level of the masses.

At this point let us examine some of the outstanding humorists of today. Let's take Will Rogers–wait a minute, let the dead rest. Anyway, Will was the type of comedian who very often attacked bankers, presidents, etc. But it was peculiar to notice that the same people whom he ridiculed very often were his hosts at lavish banquets and cocktail parties. In other words, society appreciated Will because his humor never went below the skin.

If Will had ever exposed his friends' real political life, they would not have contributed to a memorial for him–rather they would have handed him a deportation notice and the poor cowboy would have been sent back to his Golden West. The same holds true for Eddie Cantor, Peter Arno, Robert Benchley and about a thousand others who carry "light into the dark."

Around about 1929, a new institution loomed on the horizon of American life. It came at a time when people had nothing to laugh at. Breadlines were springing up and the nation was taking orders from Moscow. *Ballyhoo* was born. This magazine discovered sex in the grandest style ever imagined by any genius publisher. Where sex, in the other existing magazines, could only be understood by a lucky handful of people, Ballyhoo brought it forward in a most militant manner. History was made by a great editor who suddenly brought ladies' drawers out from their places of hiding and featured them in double spread drawings. Plumbers came into their own... bricklayers... house painters... steel workers... anyone who had an opportunity to peek into a lady's bathroom.

So great was the success of this magazine that on all sides imitators sprang up. *Bunk, Hooey, Hooey-Balooey* and *Baloney* were a few that flooded the market. The circulation was great until the country caught its breath and realized once again that sex was only an instinct. While all this was going on, it is easy to imagine that great American satirist of nearly half a century, Art Young, barricading the doorway of his cottage in Connecticut, and observing the twilight of bourgeois culture.

Art Young was probably the greatest satirist of his day. He drew for *Life, Judge, Liberator* and *Masses* many years ago. Probably the greatest of his reflections on the misery and hopelessness of life under capitalism was contained in a single drawing which Art had in the old *Masses*. The scene showed a tired worker and his wife. The man says, "Begorra, Maggie, I'm tired." She, bending over a washtub, says, "You're tired! Here I am standing over a hot stove all day, while you work in a nice cold sewer." If this was the only drawing that the old master ever did, I believe that it would have won him, some future day, immortality in a workers' America.

Today we have a new crop of satirists who, at the same time that they bite the bourgeoisie, use only their lips, but not their teeth. Peter Arno is reckoned to be the greatest of them all. There is no denying the man's greatness as an artist. He is probably the greatest producer of wash drawings today. His caricatures are ruthless in their attack, but Arno does not comprehend the significant position in society of the people whom he "attacks." He does not question once their right to rule and exploit, to create war and fascism, to bring misery and despair to the oppressed masses. Rather, he limits himself only to exposing the bourgeoisie as feeble-minded, sex-starved creatures who revel in their boudoir cavortions. Love and champagne are the only vices, to Arno, of the warmongers and makers of fascism.

Another great master of satire is Soglow. Soglow, as you know, is the creator of one of the most famous characters in American humor, the little king. In the beginning the king was quite an interesting character. Soglow began exposing the royalty as the parasitic class which it is. The king was a ridiculous character who did all sorts of stupid things. At this time, it might be mentioned that Soglow was quite close to the revolutionary movement, but gradually, as fame and fortune carried him away, the king slowly began to assume a more human appearance. Instead of being a character whom people laughed at with a feeling of contempt, the king became an object of pity, until today people smile at his antics only half-heartedly as they recognize the monarch doing familiar things that we all do. Thus, Soglow has vindicated the royalty. Even Hearst is his patron today.

Let us now discuss the comic strip which has been a form of American humor for about forty years. The first strip we shall look at is *Little Orphan Annie*. Who is this nine-year-old philosopher who has a dog named Sandy? She is a woman of the world who makes many trenchant observations on the perplexities of civilization. In January of any year Annie may be broke and hungry, but there is always February, when she will become rich. But, alas and alack, many are the moods and caprices of her great creator, who is destined to make her starve in March again. We do not know how true it is that one day the artist picked up a copy of one of the many papers in which little orphan Annie is syndicated and observed, "M'Gawd, here it is August and Annie is rich!" So the great satirist ran home and made Annie poor again. I fear that the day is not long when Annie won't live here any more.

Another strip is *Andy Gump*. Andy has been in the public eye for about twenty-five years. We find an Uncle Bim, who is a billionaire. And what, according to the creator of this strip, is the occupation of a multi-billionaire? Why, he simply gets into a limousine, rides through a ghetto, heaving tremendous bags of gold into the laps of the poor. Then there is *Jiggs*, who is supposed to typify the average American. All that this splendid example of Americanism asks is that he be allowed to eat corned beef and cabbage, and his main complaint in life is that there is always Maggie who awaits him every night with a rolling pin. Let no one of the millions of people who are disillusioned with the wretchedness of their existence under capitalism question the veracity of Jiggs. He is the ideal which the patrons of society would like the masses to pattern themselves after.

Another kind of cartoon which has suddenly been popularized is the one which deals with the police. I don't think I have to explain the function in capitalist society of the police. It will suffice to say that they are used to break strikes, to smash demonstrations of hungry workers and, in general, to protect the interests of the ruling class. However, in the Dick Tracy form of cartoon, we find that police become genuine "servants of the people," at all times eager and willing to aid the suffering citizenry. Never is Tracy the kind of a cop who breaks his club over a worker's head. Indeed, his publishers would have us believe that the police are Robin Hoods whose every campaign is against vice and crime, and are never used to terrorize the masses of people.

Then there is the *Skippy* type of cartoon. Here we find bright-faced little children who never grumble about malnutrition, or the fact that they must go to school with feet unshod, but rather philosophize on the economic traditions of the state. Thus, its creator will have his puppets discuss the size of the Navy, the strength of the Army, whether we are really prepared for Japanese invasion and, in general, are just fun-loving children with youthful fantasies and the brains of Hearst. Many strips are based on the ones which I have discussed.

What I have done here is attempt a general analysis of the humor we see in the comic supplements and the smooth paper weeklies and monthlies, as well as the kind we hear from the stage and over the radio. The men and women who draw *Jiggs, Andy Gump, Skippy, Moon Mullins* and a host of other strips... the Arnos, Soglows, Benchleys and Cantors... are all talented and funny, but... and here, I believe, is the point... their comedy is all too often a whitewash for people and conditions that, in reality, are not funny.

—A. Redfield

ALSO FROM
NEW YORK REVIEW COMICS

YELLOW NEGROES AND OTHER IMAGINARY CREATURES Yvan Alagbé

PIERO Edmond Baudoin

ALMOST COMPLETELY BAXTER Glen Baxter

AGONY Mark Beyer

MITCHUM Blutch

PEPLUM Blutch

THE GREEN HAND AND OTHER STORIES Nicole Claveloux

WHAT AM I DOING HERE? Abner Dean

THE TENDERNESS OF STONES Marion Fayolle

W THE WHORE Anke Feuchtenberger and Katrin de Vries

TROTS AND BONNIE Shary Flenniken

LETTER TO SURVIVORS Gébé

PRETENDING IS LYING Dominique Goblet

ALAY-OOP William Gropper

ALL YOUR RACIAL PROBLEMS WILL END SOON Charles Johnson

THE GULL YETIN Joe Kessler

VOICES IN THE DARK Ulli Lust

IT'S LIFE AS I SEE IT Dan Nadel (Editor)

JIMBO: ADVENTURES IN PARADISE Gary Panter

FATHER AND SON E.O. Plauen

SOFT CITY Hariton Pushwagner

THE NEW WORLD Chris Reynolds

PITTSBURGH Frank Santoro

DISCIPLINE Dash Shaw

MACDOODLE ST. Mark Alan Stamaty

SLUM WOLF Tadao Tsuge

THE MAN WITHOUT TALENT Yoshiharu Tsuge

THE PROJECTOR AND ELEPHANT Martin Vaughn-James

RETURN TO ROMANCE Ogden Whitney